ARE YOU A SPORTS NUT?

by

ERIC SCHUMAN

CCC PUBLICATIONS

Published by

CCC Publications
1111 Rancho Conejo Blvd.
Suites 411 & 412
Newbury Park, CA 91320

ISBN: 0-918259-88-6

If your local U.S. bookstore is out of stock, copies of this book may be obtained by mailing check or money order for $5.95 per book (plus $2.50 to cover postage and handling) to: CCC Publications; 1111 Rancho Conejo Blvd.; Suites 411 & 412; Newbury Park, CA 91320

Pre-publication Edition - 1/96
First Printing - 7/96

Dedicated to Yolanda, the best athlete in the whole wide . . . house!

As Chris Berman might say, special thanks to PHYS-Ed, WEST Virginia, Chia PET, Bella Lugosi, and the entire CORLEONE family!
. . . And thanks to my "entire" fan club: Andrew and Devin.

And most of all, thanks to all the major league baseball players and owners, without whose behavior, this book would not have been possible . . . or necessary!

Are YOU a sports nut? Why not try a sample quiz question:

* Saying that a sports agent is a scum-sucking parasite, would be . . .
- a) an insult to sports agents
- b) an insult to scum-sucking parasites
- c) redundant!

Too tough? Here, try another one:

* How much is Darryl Strawberry's rookie card worth today?
- a) ten dollars
- b) twenty dollars
- c) ten dollars uncut, but three thousand bucks street value

Still stumped? Then start reading . . . and GET IN THE GAME!

TABLE OF CONTENTS

Chapter One: BASEBALL
(a.k.a. "the Billionaire Boys' Club")

BASEBALL'S FIERCEST RIVALRY

TRUTH IN ADVERTISING

FIELDER'S CHOICE

DOING THE WAVE IN LOS ANGELES

POULTRY-LEAGUE BASEBALL

...AND AFTER THREE-AND-A-HALF INNINGS, IT'S THE PAMPERED MULTIMILLIONAIRES FIVE, AND THE EGOMANIACAL CRYBABIES THREE.
VISITORS
PAMPERED MULTIMILLIONAIRES
1 2 3 4 5 6 7 8 9
1 0 2 0
0 2 3

BASEBALL'S NEW SALARY CAP

BASEBALL QUIZ

1. Name the official movie of major league baseball:
   a) Easy Money
   b) Other People's Money
   c) The Money Pit

2. The best thing that can be said for baseball is:
   a) It's still America's pastime
   b) It's still basically the same game Babe Ruth played
   c) At least Don King's not involved!

3. In baseball, each player receives a maximum of:
   a) 3 strikes, 4 balls, for 3 outs
   b) 2 strikes, 3 balls, for 4 outs
   c) no exact number, but for the players to be OUT
      so much on so many STRIKES, they sure must
      have alot of BALLS!

4. The New York Mets are like "Saturday Night Live" in what way?
   a) They're both filmed live
   b) They're both from New York
   c) They both have lots of errors, but are still good for a few laughs

4. The New York Mets are like "Saturday Night Live" in what way?
   a) They're both filmed live
   b) They're both from New York
   c) They both have lots of errors, but are still good for a few laughs

5. What did Hideo Nomo say upon learning he'd been selected National League Rookie of the Year?
   a)
   b)
   c)

THE TV GENERATION

OFF-SIDES

... HE'S AT THE 35...THE 40...THE 45...THE 50...THE 45...THE 40...THE 35...
DEAR— WHY DID THAT MAN TURN AROUND AND START RUNNING THE OTHER WAY?

...THERE'S BEEN SOME TALK THAT YOUR FIRST-ROUND DRAFT PICK HASN'T BEEN LIVING UP TO EXPECTATIONS SO FAR...
HEY, THAT KID'S GONNA BE A STAR– HE MAY BE A LITTLE RAW, BUT HE'S GOT THE STRENGTH OF TEN MEN!
...UNFORTUNATELY, THOSE TEN ARE WOODY ALLEN, MICHAEL JACKSON, ANDY ROONEY, BARRY MANILOW, TOMMY TUNE, KIETH RICHARDS, BOY GEORGE,...

FOOTBALL QUIZ:

1. What does it mean when a defense overloads one side?
    a) They anticipate the play going to that side
    b) The other team's tendencies lean toward that side
    c) William "The Refrigerator" Perry is on that side

2. "Cross-country hiking" is...
    a) A great way to see nature while getting an aerobic workout
    b) A perfect combination of mountain climbing and leisure walking
    c) When the center snaps the ball way over the head of the punter!

3. Which of Fox TV's innovations brought the most new fans to its NFL telecasts:
    a) the Overhead End-Zone-Cam
    b) the Helmet-Cam
    c) the Pulled-Groin-Cam

4. The Raiders are the official team of:
    a) Los Angeles
    b) Oakland
    c) Allied Van Lines

5. Who was O.J. Simpson's coach at USC?
    a) John Robinson
    b) John McKay
    c) We don't really know, we just didn't want this to be the
       only book published in this century that didn't mention O.J.!

Chapter Three: BASKETBALL
(the REAL Hoop Scoop!)

HOOP DREAMS

THAT'S WHAT I LOVE ABOUT BASKETBALL — IT'S THE ONE GAME LEFT WHERE WE AMERICANS ARE STILL BEST IN THE WORLD!
NBA All ★ Star Weekend
...VLADE DIVAC TAKES THE BALL FROM HAKEEM OLAJOWAN AND PASSES TO DETLEF SCHREMPF, WHO IS BEING GUARDED BY DIKEMBE MOTUMBO...

CHARGING

BASKETBALL QUIZ

1. Manute Bol once missed two weeks of the NBA season when he...
   a) pulled a hamstring
   b) sprained an ankle
   c) snapped in two

2. No NBA team can be considered truly great until it has...
   a) beaten the defending NBA champion
   b) repeated as NBA champion
   c) pissed off Spike Lee

3. Mugsy Bogues' career goal is to some day be...
   a) on an NBA championship team
   b) elected to the NBA All Star Game
   c) called for goal-tending

4. Dennis Rodman's goal is to attain...
   a) a third championship ring
   b) a fourth All Star ring
   c) a fifth nipple ring

5. Match the NBA player with the movie he starred in:
   a) Shaquille O'Neal   1) Blue Chips
   b) Larry Bird   2) White Men Can't Jump
   c) Spud Web   3) Little Big Man
   d) Dennis Rodman's hair   4) The Color Purple

Chapter FOOOOOOOOOOOORE!; GOLF

SHANK

BALL FOUR

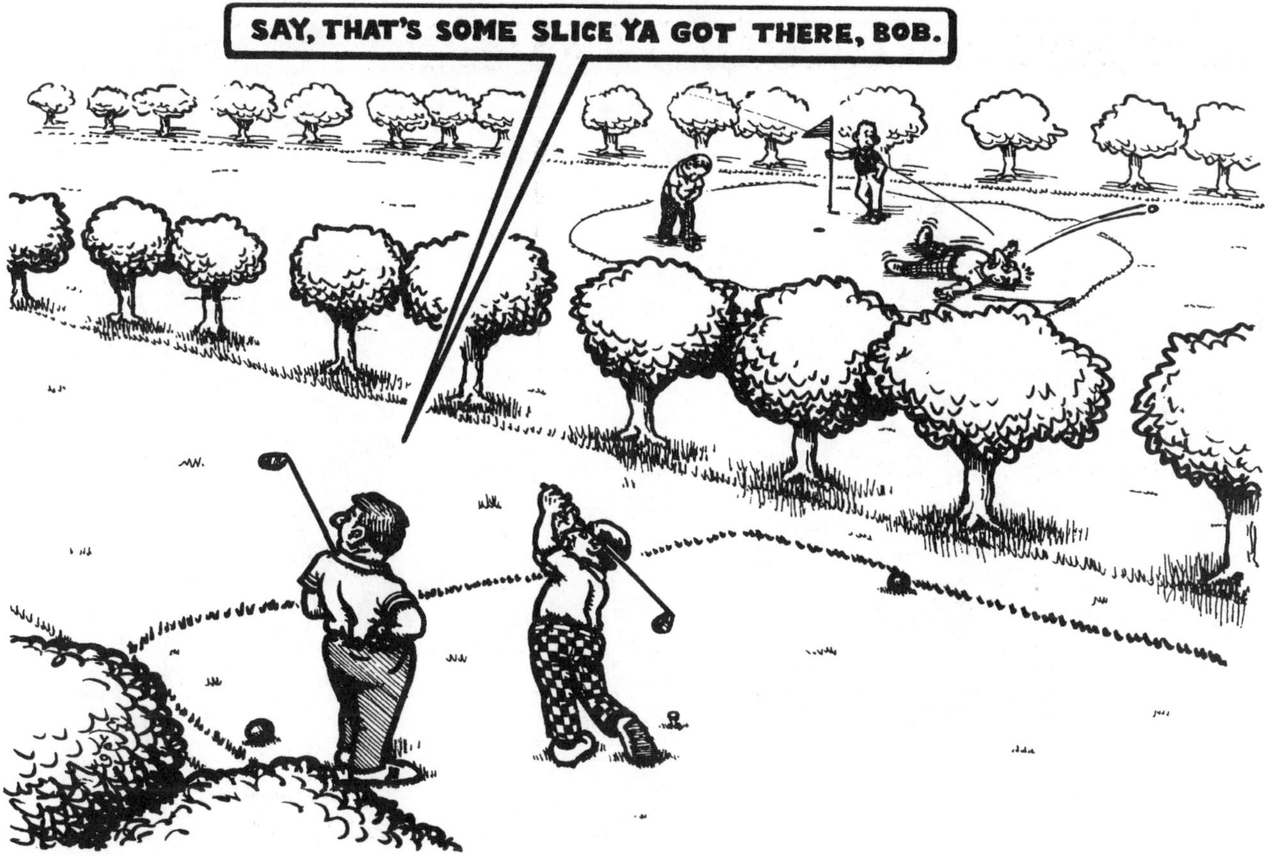
SAY, THAT'S SOME SLICE YA GOT THERE, BOB.

DOUBLE BOGEY

GOLF QUIZ

1. Golf is very popular on television in spite of the fact that...
    a) the ball is too small to track on camera
    b) the crowds often obscure the camera's view
    c) they all dress like such dorks

2. A triple-eagle on a par-five means...
    a) a hole in one
    b) a score of two
    c) John Daly hit it

3. If one is having a particularly bad day on the golf course, one's best club usually will be...
    a) the sand wedge
    b) the putter
    c) wrapped around a tree

4. The difference between Jack Nicklaus and Jack Nicholson is...
    a) One is a golden bear, the other is a wolf
    b) One gets a lot of birdies, the other flew over the cuckoo's nest
    c) One: Uses golf club on par four, plays fine
        The other: Uses golf club on car door, pays fine

5. Although America is the preeminent practitioner of golf today, the sport was actually invented by...
    a) the British
    b) the Scottish
    c) the Devil

Chapter Five: TENNIS
(and other sports that raise a RACQUET!)

SPORTS INJURIES

TENNIS ELBOW

PING-PONG BALLS

58

59

DOUBLE FAULT

PRINCE RACKET

TABLE TENNIS

TENNIS QUIZ

1. **In tennis, zero plus one equals:**
    a) one
    b) zero
    c) fifteen (?!?)

2. **The term "fifteen-love" means that...**
    a) the server has lost the first point of that game
    b) the receiver has an excellent chance to break serve
    c) Joey Buttafuoco is probably headed for jail again

3. **What is the best evidence that the club tennis pro is a very influential person?**
    a) Women who are only casual tennis fans become avid enthusiasts after only a few lessons with him
    b) Women who'd shown little tennis appitude become highly accomplished after extended training with him
    c) When these women have babies, the babies usually look like him

4. **How is tennis like poker?**
    a) they both require great concentration
    b) they both depend on long-term strategy
    c) the one with the most aces usually wins

5. **From the way that tennis is scored, we may safely assume that the rules for tennis were invented by...**
    a) Albert Einstein
    b) Albert Brooks
    c) Foster Broooks
    d) accident

67

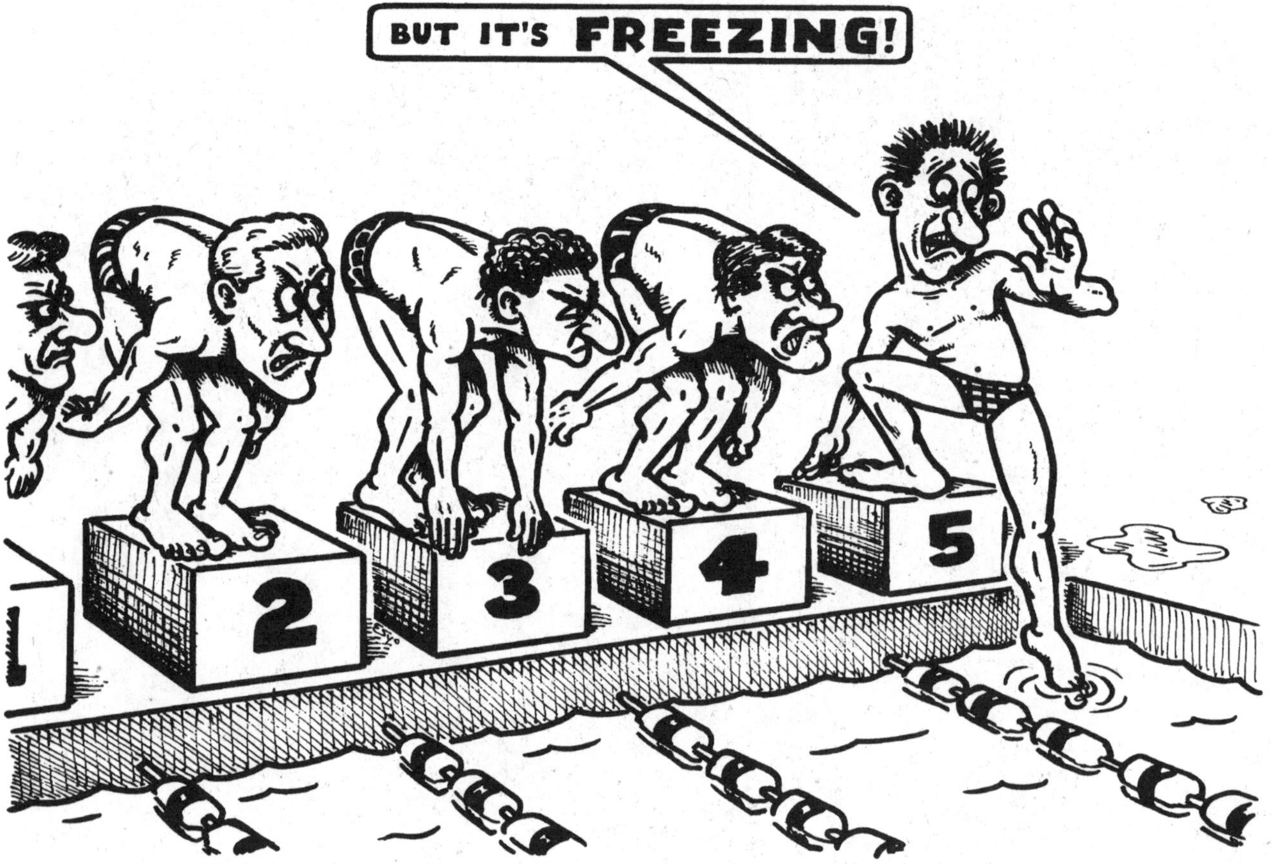
BUT IT'S FREEZING!
2
3
4
5

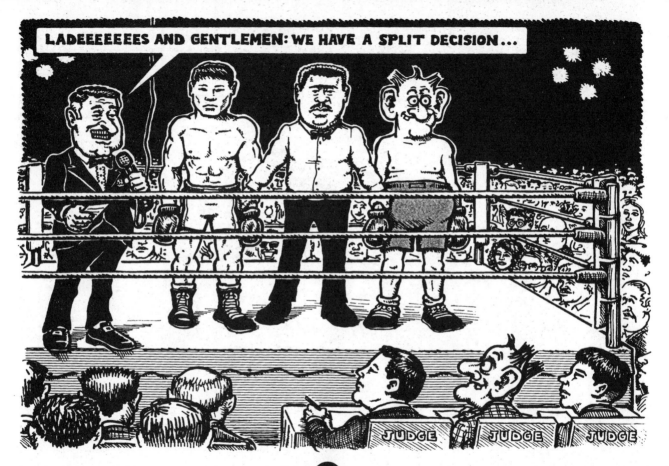

...OF COURSE, EVER SINCE THE NANCY-TANYA EPISODE, THE SKATERS HAVE FELT THE NEED FOR A BIT MORE PROTECTION...
USA
I ♥ SKATING

OLYMPICS QUIZ

1. **The Olympic Hammer-Throw is usually won by...**
   a) a Russian
   b) a German
   c) a carpenter who's just banged his thumb

2. **The Pole Vault is:**
   a) the greatest vertical-distance event in the Olympics
   b) one of the ten events in the Olympic Decathlon
   c) where the former mayor of Warsaw is buried

3. **The most coveted prize in the Olympics is...**
   a) the Gold medal
   b) the Silver medal
   c) the "Now I'm going to Disney World" spot

4. **Which Olympic event has long been dominated by the French?**
   a) Team cycling
   b) The downhill slalom
   c) The 100-yard surrender

5. **The difference between Olympic Basketball and NBA Basketball is the presence of...**
   a) multi-lingual referees
   b) the international 3-point line
   c) white guys

Chapter Seven: CONTACT SPORTS
(including Karate, Judo, and California Freeway-driving!)

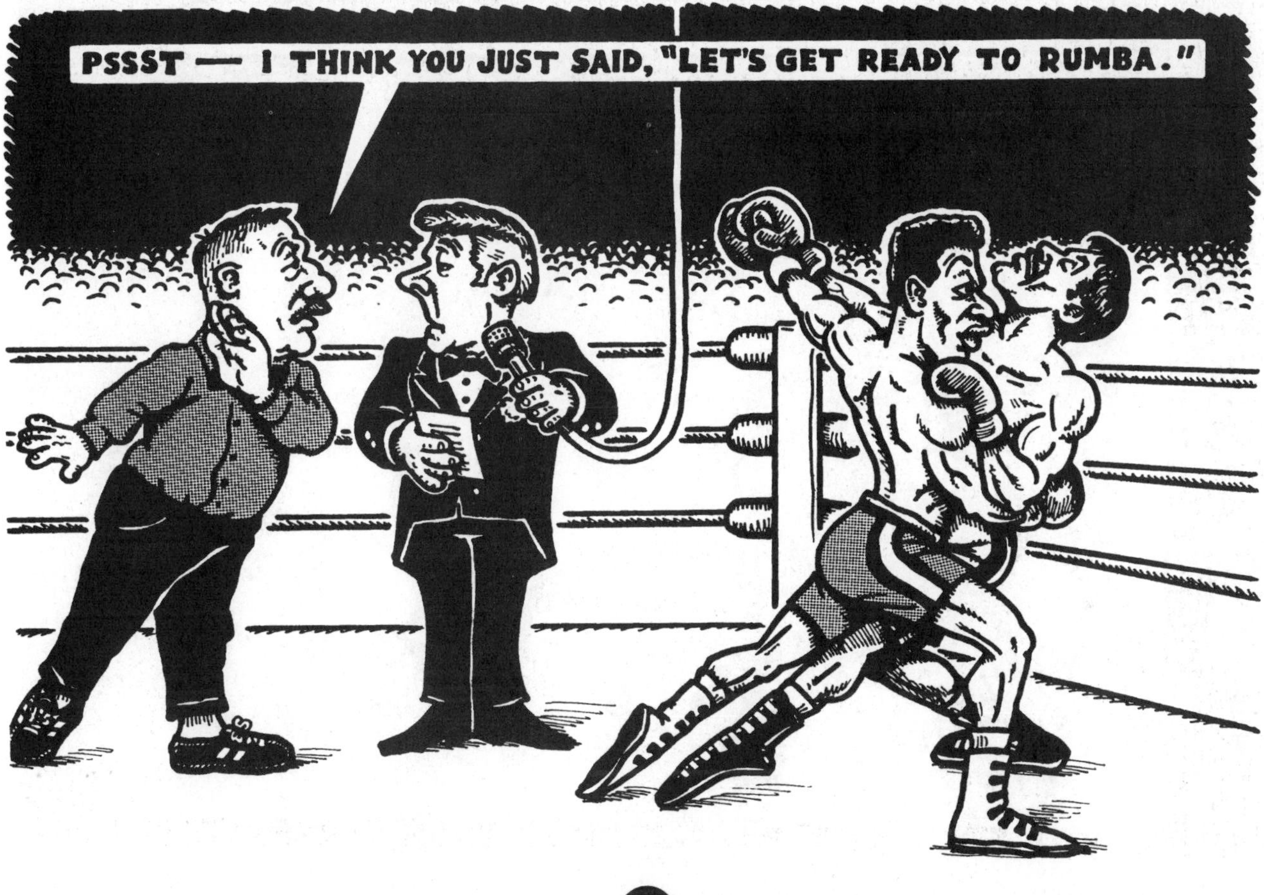
PSSST — I THINK YOU JUST SAID, "LET'S GET READY TO RUMBA."

SELF-DEFENSE TECHNIQUES:

KARATE

JUDO

SUSHI

SCENE FROM "ROCKY **XVII** — ROCKY VS. BULWINKLE"

KARATE POSITION:

CORRECT

INCORRECT

CONTACT SPORTS QUIZ

1. **Is golf considered a contact sport?**
   a) yes, because the club makes contact with the ball
   b) no, because there is no physical contact between players
   c) only when Gerald Ford is playing

2. **In prison, Mike Tyson's nickname was...**
   a) Iron-Bars Mike
   b) the Jailhouse Rock
   c) Mister Tyson, sir

3. **Which of George Foreman's sons is the eldest?**
   a) George
   b) George
   c) George

4. **Who is known as "Hands of Stone"?**
   a) Roberto Duran
   b) Sonny Liston
   c) The New York Mets' infield

5. **True or False: One of the skills involved in Karate is ball-handling.**
   a) True
   b) False
   c) Insert your own punch-line here

Chapter Eight: THE GREAT OUTDOORS
(better known as, "What's This Rash?")

KINDS OF BEARS

KODIAK   **POLAR**

KODAK   **POLAROID**

HUNTING TERMS

GRIZZLY BEAR

GRIZZLY, BARE

THE MOST POPULAR KINDS OF BAIT

LIVE BAIT   CRANK BAIT   JAIL BAIT

THE GREAT OUTDOORS QUIZ

1. The most popular activity at camp is:
   a) the campfire
   b) the marshmallow roast
   c) going on panty-raids

2. The movie "The Great Outdoors" was about...
   a) a family camping trip
   b) cabin fever
   c) two hours too long

3. When a man marches off for the day with fishing gear in hand and a confident smile on his face, the experienced wife knows she can plan on making_____ for dinner.
   a) fresh rainbow trout
   b) fried catfish
   c) reservations

4. When camping, if approached by a bear, always be sure...
   a) you have a can of mace nearby
   b) you're not sleeping in the same area as your provisions
   c) you can outrun at least one other camper

5. One sure sign of acute hypothermia is when a member of a mountain climbing expedition begins...
   a) shivering uncontrollably
   b) turning blue
   c) going on panty-raids

Chapter Nine: WOMEN
(You know, the sports you only see on ESPN2!)

WOMEN IN SPORTS QUIZ

1. Complete the following old saying "Women--ya can't live with 'em,...."
   - a) ya can't live without 'em
   - b) so you may as well marry 'em
   - c) after they've beaten you at golf!

2. If Florence Griffith-Joyner were cloned with Jackie Joyner-Kersey, the result would be...
   - a) Aranxta-Sanchez-Vicario
   - b) Florence-Jackie-Griffith-Joyner-Kersey-Fawcett-Majors
   - c) too long to print in a paperback

3. When one woman tells another "If you don't mind my saying, you seem to be having a bad hair day", this is their version of...
   - a) friendly advice
   - b) a helpful hints
   - c) trash-talking

4. Biologists say women would already have surpassed men in marathon competition except for the fact that...
   - a) Men naturally have more fat to burn
   - b) Men's larger bodies carry more much-needed water
   - c) Men rarely stop to shop in mid-race

5. A women's pro baseball league could be quite profitable due to...
   - a) high interest sparked by the movie "A League of Their Own"
   - b) fans' perception that men's baseball has become too greedy for mass appeal
   - c) all the money they'd save on protective cups

WELL, YOUR FOLLOW-THROUGH COULD STILL USE SOME WORK... BUT YOUR SCORE'S IMPROVING.
COACH

SOCCER TEAM MEAL

STOLE
A
BASE

ROBBED
SOMEONE
OF A HIT

SHOT
A
BIRDIE

DRAG RACING

POOL SHARK

TOP TEN SPORTS TERMS THAT SOUND DIRTY BUT REALLY AREN'T:

10. CLEAN AND JERK
9. BALL HANDLING
8. FAT LEVER
7. SLIDING IN HARD
6. DEEP ZONE
5. GETTING TO THIRD BASE
4. SCREWBALL
3. THE HIGH HARD ONE
2. BLOWING A SAVE
1. DICK BUTKUS

"ARE YOU A SPORTS NUT?" FINAL QUIZ:
How many of these statements describe you?
(Correct responses are on the next page.)

1. You can't go to bed until you hear the final scores of all the late games, even though you don't know who's playing.

2. Every day you get into the exact same argument with your spouse: "Oh yeah? Well to me, watching soap operas and talk shows every day is stupid!"

3. You stay awake during the entire Super Bowl.

4. You can't name the Secretary of State, but you can name the starting five for the New Jersey Nets.

5. You get into heated arguments about who would win in a fist fight: Roger Clemens or Bernie Kosar.

6. Although you've heard that you should think about sports during sex to delay sexual climax, that trick doesn't work for you, because thinking about sports just gets you more excited.

7. Your TV has Picture-in-Picture, and both screens are always tuned to ballgames.

8. You miss Howard Cosell.

9. If you're standing right next to the trash can with a piece of garbage, you'll back up ten feet and go for the jump shot.

10. You spend hours thinking up Chris Berman-style nicknames for famous people. Like George "Beat around the" Bush, or Vincent "Look at that" Van Gogh.

"ARE YOU A SPORTS NUT?" CORRECT RESPONSES:
(Results are on the next page.)

1. Who cares who's playing—there might be a triple play or a brawl on the highlights, and if you went to bed, you'd miss it!

2. The only difference is, when there's two minutes left on "Days of Our Lives", it's over in two minutes, but two minutes left in the Lakers-Knicks game could take an hour and a half!

3. If you stay awake for the entire Super Bowl, you're definitely not on the Buffalo Bills!

4. If you can name BOTH the Secretary of State and the Nets' starting five, you're Jeopardy material. If you can't name either, you're Dan Quayle.

5. The correct answer is Bernie Kosar.

6. Just try not to think about SEX during SPORTS...especially if you're a swimmer, and you're wearing a Speedo!

7. Now if they only had Picture-In-Picture-In-Picture, you could also keep an eye on that exciting pro-beach volleyball semi-final match on ESPN-21

8. If you've ever missed Howard Cosell...take better aim next time!

9. One warning: When shooting a half-eaten pizza slice at the family room waste basket, go for the swish, not the bank shot.

10. You really should try to do something better with your time. (Just some friendly advice from your author, Eric "You better take this broken heel to the" Schu-man.)

"ARE YOU A SPORTS NUT?" SCORING:

0-4 What are you, a little girlie-man?

5-8 CASUAL SPORTS FAN. Like the other guys you come into work saying "How 'bout that game last night!" But in your case, you're probably referring to last night's **Wheel of Fortune.**

9-12 AVID SPORTS FAN. You get more excited by the spread in the Steelers-Browns game than by the one in Penthouse.

13-15 SPORTS ADDICT. You cannot live without your sports. Can you imagine, no sports, 24 hours a day, 365 days a year? Why it would be like...
CBS!

*However for the TRUE test, go back to question #5. You see, it's a trick question. Bernie Kosar would never fight Roger Clemens, they're not even in the same sport, they'd never risk injuring their throwing arms,... heck, they probably have never even met! But if you cared enough to look at the answer and say, "Kosar? No way! Clemens would cream him!"... Congratulations: You, my friend, are an official, regulation-weight, score-card-keeping, update-watching, season-ticket-holding, stat-knowing, box-score-reading, tail-gating

SPORTS NUT!

TITLES BY CCC PUBLICATIONS

Retail $4.99
"?" book
POSITIVELY PREGNANT
SIGNS YOUR SEX LIFE IS DEAD
WHY MEN DON'T HAVE A CLUE
40 AND HOLDING YOUR OWN
CAN SEX IMPROVE YOUR GOLF?
THE COMPLETE BOOGER BOOK
THINGS YOU CAN DO WITH A USELESS MAN
FLYING FUNNIES
MARITAL BLISS & OXYMORONS
THE VERY VERY SEXY ADULT DOT-TO-DOT BOOK
THE DEFINITIVE FART BOOK
THE COMPLETE WIMP'S GUIDE TO SEX
THE CAT OWNER'S SHAPE UP MANUAL
PMS CRAZED: TOUCH ME AND I'LL KILL YOU!
RETIRED: LET THE GAMES BEGIN
MALE BASHING: WOMEN'S FAVORITE PASTIME
THE OFFICE FROM HELL
FOOD & SEX
FITNESS FANATICS
YOUNGER MEN ARE BETTER THAN RETIN-A
BUT OSSIFER, IT'S NOT MY FAULT

Retail $4.95
1001 WAYS TO PROCRASTINATE
THE WORLD'S GREATEST PUT-DOWN LINES
HORMONES FROM HELL II
SHARING THE ROAD WITH IDIOTS
THE GREATEST ANSWERING MACHINE MESSAGES
   OF ALL TIME
WHAT DO WE DO NOW?? (A Guide For New Parents)
HOW TO TALK YOU WAY OUT OF A TRAFFIC TICKET
THE BOTTOM HALF (How To Spot Incompetent
   Professionals)
LIFE'S MOST EMBARRASSING MOMENTS
HOW TO ENTERTAIN PEOPLE YOU HATE
YOUR GUIDE TO CORPORATE SURVIVAL
THE SUPERIOR PERSON'S GUIDE TO EVERYDAY
   IRRITATIONS
GIFTING RIGHT

Retail $3.95
YOU KNOW YOU'RE AN OLD FART WHEN...
NO HANG-UPS
NO HANG-UPS II
NO HANG-UPS III
HOW TO SUCCEED IN SINGLES BARS
HOW TO GET EVEN WITH YOUR EXES
TOTALLY OUTRAGEOUS BUMPER-SNICKERS ($2.95)

TITLES BY CCC PUBLICATIONS

Retail $5.95
LITTLE INSTRUCTION BOOK OF THE RICH & FAMOUS
GETTING EVEN WITH THE ANSWERING MACHINE
ARE YOU A SPORTS NUT?
MEN ARE PIGS / WOMEN ARE BITCHES
50 WAYS TO HUSTLE YOUR FRIENDS ($5.99)
HORMONES FROM HELL
HUSBANDS FROM HELL
KILLER BRAS & Other Hazards Of The 50's
IT'S BETTER TO BE OVER THE HILL THAN UNDER IT
HOW TO REALLY PARTY!!!
WORK SUCKS!
THE PEOPLE WATCHER'S FIELD GUIDE
THE UNOFFICIAL WOMEN'S DIVORCE GUIDE
THE ABSOLUTE LAST CHANCE DIET BOOK
FOR MEN ONLY (How To Survive Marriage)
THE UGLY TRUTH ABOUT MEN
NEVER A DULL CARD
RED HOT MONOGAMY
   (In Just 60 Seconds A Day) ($6.95)

NO HANG-UPS – CASSETTES Retail $4.98
Vol. I: GENERAL MESSAGES (Female)
Vol. I: GENERAL MESSAGES (Male)
Vol. II: BUSINESS MESSAGES (Female)
Vol. II: BUSINESS MESSAGES (Male)
Vol. III: 'R' RATED MESSAGES (Female)
Vol. III: 'R' RATED MESSAGES (Male)
Vol. IV: SOUND EFFECTS ONLY
Vol. V: CELEBRI-TEASE